NATIONAL GEOGRAPHIC
Forces of Nature

GENRE Folk Tale

Read to find out how Paul and Babe changed the land.

PAUL BUNYAN AND BABE THE BLUE OX

RETOLD BY ROGER BACH

ILLUSTRATED BY ROBB MOMMAERTS

BABE THE BLUE OX
PAUL BUNYAN
LUMBERJACKS WERE BUSY IN THE 1800S. THE UNITED STATES WAS GROWING FASTER THAN CORN IN IOWA. A LOT OF LUMBER WAS NEEDED TO BUILD NEW THINGS. LUMBERJACKS OFTEN LIVED FAR FROM TOWN IN LOGGING CAMPS.
THEY TOLD EACH OTHER STORIES DURING THE LONG WINTERS. SOME WERE ABOUT A GIANT LUMBERJACK NAMED PAUL BUNYAN. THE STORIES WERE LATER PUBLISHED. NEW STORIES WERE ADDED.

IN THE YEAR OF TWO WINTERS . . .
IT WAS SO COLD THAT WHEN THE LUMBERJACKS WENT OUTSIDE, THEIR NOSES TURNED BLUE. LUCKILY PAUL DIDN'T MIND THE BITTER COLD. OTHERWISE BABE MIGHT NOT HAVE BEEN RESCUED THAT DAY IN MINNESOTA
WHAT ARE THOSE, BEANPOLES?
SNORT
YOU POOR BABE. YOU'RE COLDER THAN AN ICEBERG IN THE SHADE. I'LL CALL YOU "BABE THE BLUE OX."

THAT SPRING, BABE GREW AND GREW.
APPLE FLAPJACKS ARE OFF THE MENU!
YUM!
BABE HELPED THE LUMBERJACKS WITH CHORES.
I HOPE I GET A SNACK BEFORE THESE DRY.
IT TOOK THE BLACKSMITH A YEAR TO MAKE BABE'S "OX SHOES." EACH SHOE WEIGHED MORE THAN 12 MEN.
BABE COULD EASILY PULL 50 LOGS WHEN HE WAS GROWN. AT FIRST THE LUMBERJACKS DIDN'T KNOW THE SOUND OF BABE'S STOMPING.
IS THAT THUNDER?

THE PAN FOR PAUL'S WAGON-WHEEL PANCAKES WAS BIG ENOUGH TO **BOAST** ABOUT. IT WAS HEAVIER THAN A RAILROAD CAR.
MEN SKATED ACROSS THE PAN ON BUTTER TO GREASE IT. THEN SOMEONE PULLED A ROPE TO POUR THE BATTER.
BE CAREFUL! DON'T COOK YOUR FEET!
WATCH OUT!
WHOA!

PAUL AND BABE FORM THE 10,000 LAKES . . .
IN THE SUMMER, PAUL AND BABE PLAYED GAMES OUTSIDE. ONCE PAUL TRIED TO TEACH BABE TO PLAY FETCH.
CATCH MY LONG TOSS!
THEN BABE TAUGHT PAUL HOW TO WRESTLE.
THEY WRESTLED UP AND DOWN MINNESOTA. NOBODY KNOWS WHO WON.
NOW I HAVE YOU!
I DOUBT IT!
LATER A THUNDERSTORM FLOODED THE LANDFORMS THEY LEFT BEHIND. THAT'S HOW MINNESOTA'S 10,000 LAKES WERE FORMED.

PAUL MAKES THE GREAT LAKES . . .
DURING THE SUMMER OF NO RAIN, ALL 10,000 LAKES DRIED UP. PAUL AND BABE CROSSED THE BORDER INTO WISCONSIN TO FIND WATER.
THEY HAD TO DIG TO FIND IT.
NOT TO BOAST, BUT I CAN OUT-DIG AN ARMY OF GOPHERS.
PAUL AND BABE DUG FIVE HUGE HOLES BORDERING EIGHT STATES AND CANADA. BUT THEY DIDN'T FIND WATER.
PAUL TRIED ONCE MORE. HE SWUNG HIS AX WITH SUCH FORCE THE GROUND SHOOK. WATER SHOT UP LIKE A GEYSER.
IT FILLED THE FIVE HUGE HOLES AND FORMED THE GREAT LAKES.

PAUL AND BABE FORM THE MISSISSIPPI . . .
ONCE PAUL WANTED TO ICE THE LOGGING ROADS. HE MADE A BARREL SO HUGE IT TOOK HALF A DAY TO WALK AROUND IT. THEN HE FILLED IT WITH WATER.
PAUL COULD BARELY LIFT THE BARREL, BUT HE GOT BABE TO PULL IT.
YOU'LL GET AN ORCHARD'S WORTH OF APPLES FOR THIS.
ONLY 30 MILES MORE!
SNORT!
BABE TRIPPED. THE BARREL FELL AND BROKE OPEN.
HUMPH!
THE WATER FLOWED TO THE SEA, AND THAT'S HOW THE MISSISSIPPI RIVER WAS FORMED.

PAUL FORMS THE GRAND CANYON . . .
PAUL AND BABE HEADED SOUTHWEST. AT THE ARIZONA BORDER, IT WAS HOT ENOUGH TO FRY A FLAPJACK ON PAUL'S AX.
I HAVEN'T SEEN LAND THIS DRY SINCE THE SUMMER OF NO RAIN.
WATCH YOUR STEP. YOU DON'T WANT TO TRIP ON A CANYON.
I MISS THE SNOW.
PAUL AND BABE WEREN'T USED TO THE HEAT.
I WISH THIS AX WEREN'T SO HEAVY. I'M STRONG, BUT THE SUN IS STRONGER.

Check In What were the forces of nature in these tales?

 Read to find out how water shapes Earth's surface.

Water's Might

by Brian Phelps

Water can be one of nature's strongest **forces.** Rivers, oceans, and ice build and destroy **landforms.** Water can wear down mountains. It can carve valleys. It can move giant rocks. These changes can happen quickly or take thousands of years.

Spencer Glacier in Alaska's Kenai Mountains

Earth's Icy Past

Almost one-third of Earth's land was covered by **glaciers** 20,000 years ago. Glaciers are huge, slow-moving sheets of ice. They form where snow builds up over time. The heavy top snow squeezes the bottom snow into ice. This heavy ice flows downhill. Some glaciers can move several meters a day.

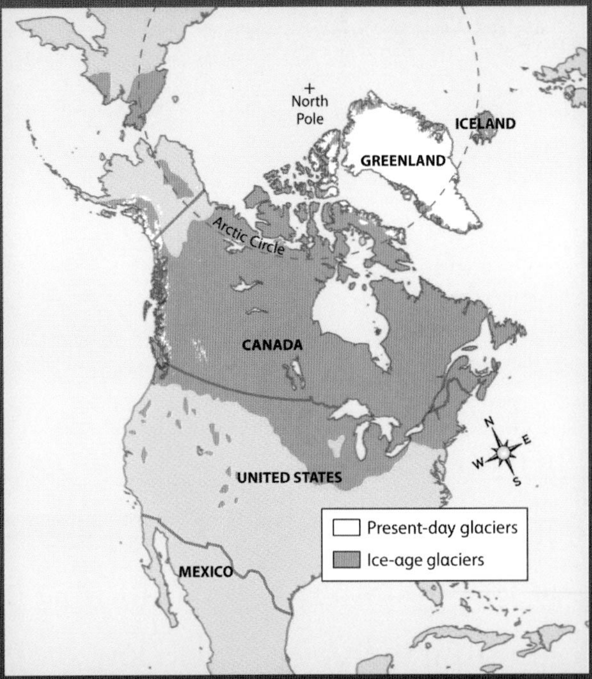

Glaciers spread and shrank several times during the last ice age. In some places, the ice was more than 3 kilometers (almost 2 miles) thick! Today's glaciers cover Antarctica, most of Greenland, and many high mountains.

The Great Lakes

Over time, ice-age glaciers changed North America. The glaciers eroded the land under them as they moved. **Erosion** is the movement of rock and soil. The glaciers caused erosion by carrying sediment from one place to another. Sediment is loose soil, sand, gravel, and rocks.

When the glaciers melted, they dropped the sediment. **Deposition** is the dropping of sediment in a new place. The sediment from these glaciers formed hills and other landforms. Water from melting ice filled low spots. This formed the Great Lakes. Together the Great Lakes make up the largest surface area of fresh water in the world.

HOW DID LAKE MICHIGAN FORM?

1 MILLION YEARS AGO

The area now covered by Lake Michigan was a lowland. It had valleys and rivers.

20,000 YEARS AGO

Erosion by earlier glaciers had gouged out the land to form a basin. A basin is a very wide area that is deeper than the surrounding land.

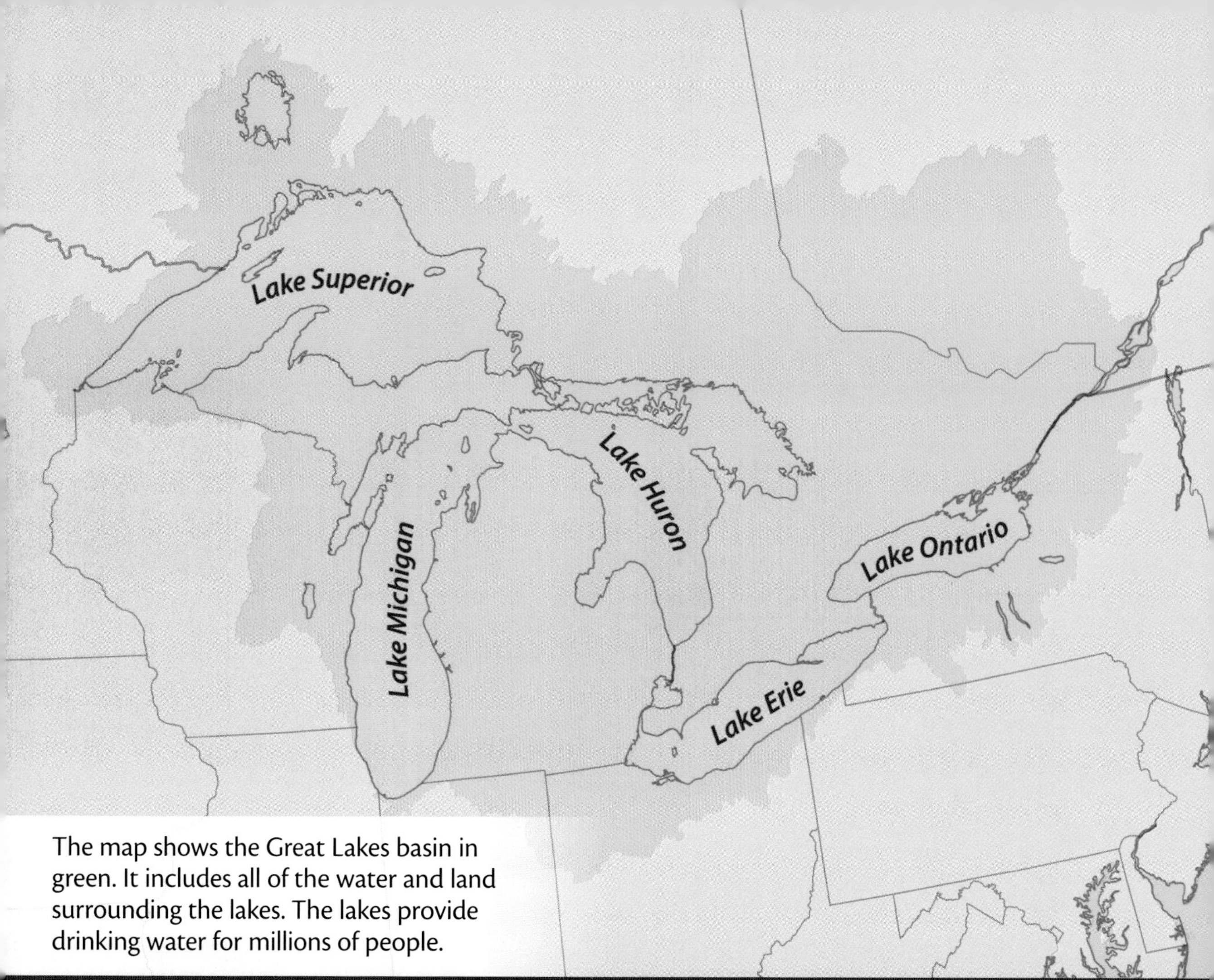

The map shows the Great Lakes basin in green. It includes all of the water and land surrounding the lakes. The lakes provide drinking water for millions of people.

14,000 YEARS AGO

The last glaciers slowly melted. Lake Michigan began to form. Deposition along the edge of the ice sheet helped trap water in the basin.

3,000 YEARS AGO TO PRESENT

Lake Michigan started to reach its present-day shape and size. It is the second-largest Great Lake. Water from four states drains into it.

Mighty Glaciers, Many Lakes

Minnesota, Michigan, and Wisconsin have thousands of lakes. Many came from glaciers. These ice sheets scraped the land as they moved. The ice pushed piles of soil and rock into hills and ridges. It carved deep holes in the land. The holes filled with water when the glaciers melted.

Minnesota has more than 12,000 lakes.

Melting glaciers filled Minnesota's lakes about 8,000 years ago. Minnesota has more than 53,000 square kilometers (20,500 square miles) of surface water. That's why Minnesota is called "Land of 10,000 Lakes"!

Rivers at Work

Like glaciers, rivers are a force of nature. Rivers are large streams of flowing water. They shape the land through erosion and deposition. Rivers carve out valleys and cut **canyons.** They carry a lot of sediment. Some rivers flow into a lake or ocean. There the sediment can build up to form a delta. A delta is new land that forms at the end of a river.

A river delta in Lake Chiemsee, Germany

Most rivers start small. They get larger by collecting more and more water. All rivers flow downhill. Fast rivers erode more land than slow rivers. But all rivers pick up sediment. They carry the sediment to other areas. That's how rivers change Earth's surface.

A Grand Landform

The Colorado River winds through the Grand Canyon. The river shaped the Grand Canyon partly through erosion. It cut the canyon into cliffs and slopes.

The Colorado River began forming the Grand Canyon millions of years ago. The river slowly wore away the rock walls. The canyon got deeper and wider. Now parts of the Grand Canyon are more than a mile deep!

1,840–270
MILLION YEARS AGO

Water and wind deposited new layers of sediment. The sediment layers gradually became rock layers.

The Colorado River flows along the bottom of the Grand Canyon.

HOW DID THE GRAND CANYON FORM?

70–40
MILLION YEARS AGO

Forces below Earth's surface pushed up an area of land bigger than New Mexico. It was raised thousands of meters.

5–6
MILLION YEARS AGO

The Colorado River began to flow. The high elevation allowed the river to flow very fast. The river cut deeper into the rock.

Present

The Colorado continued eroding rock. Parts of the canyon walls fell inward. They were also eroded. Today the canyon is very deep and wide.

The Mighty Mississippi

The Mississippi River flows from Minnesota's Lake Itasca to the Gulf of Mexico. It is one of the largest and longest rivers in North America. It is shallow at Lake Itasca and very deep near the Gulf. How does it grow so large?

Other rivers and streams empty into the Mississippi. Rainy weather adds even more. If the river gets too full, it flows onto nearby land. This nearby land is called a floodplain.

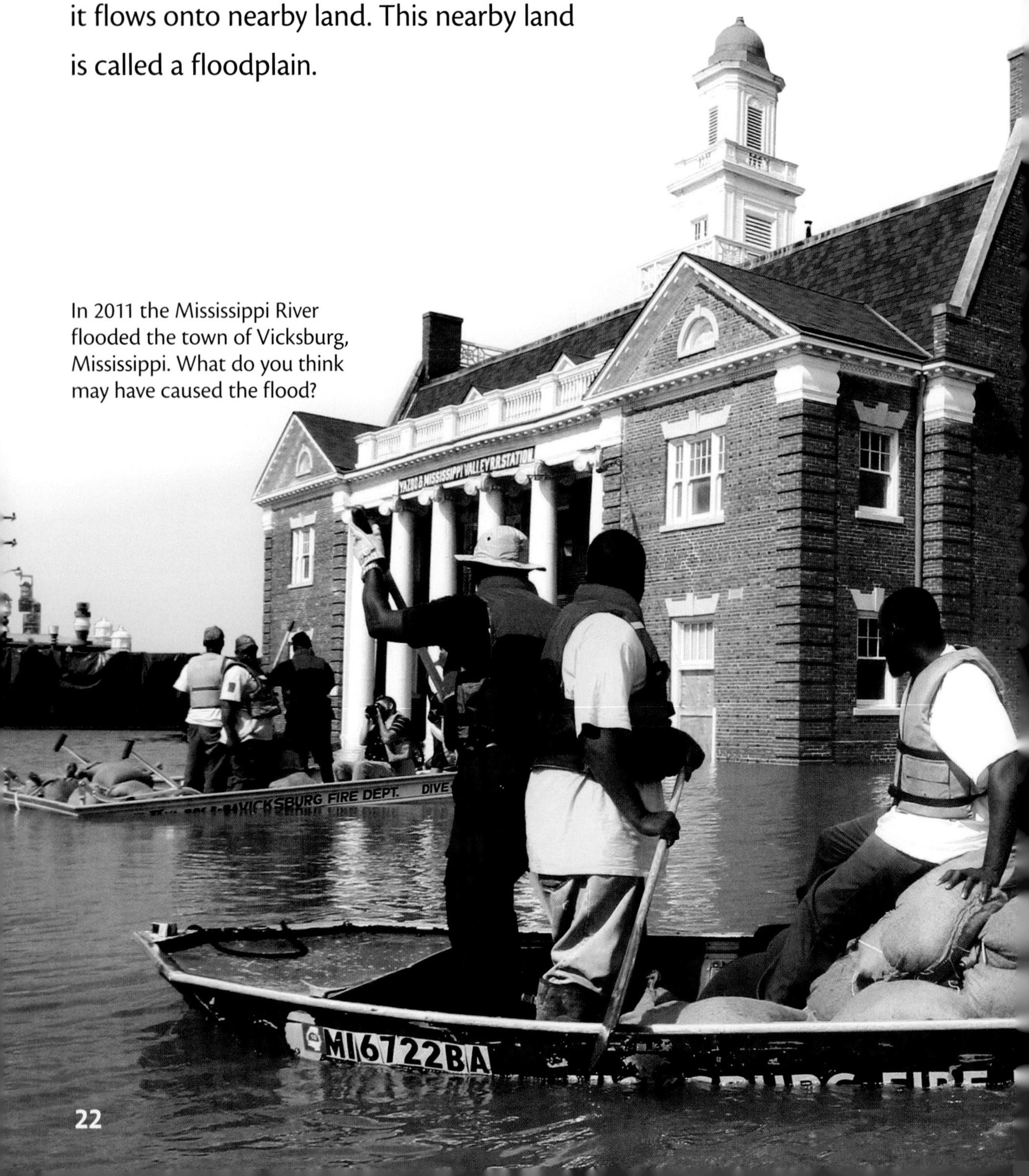

In 2011 the Mississippi River flooded the town of Vicksburg, Mississippi. What do you think may have caused the flood?

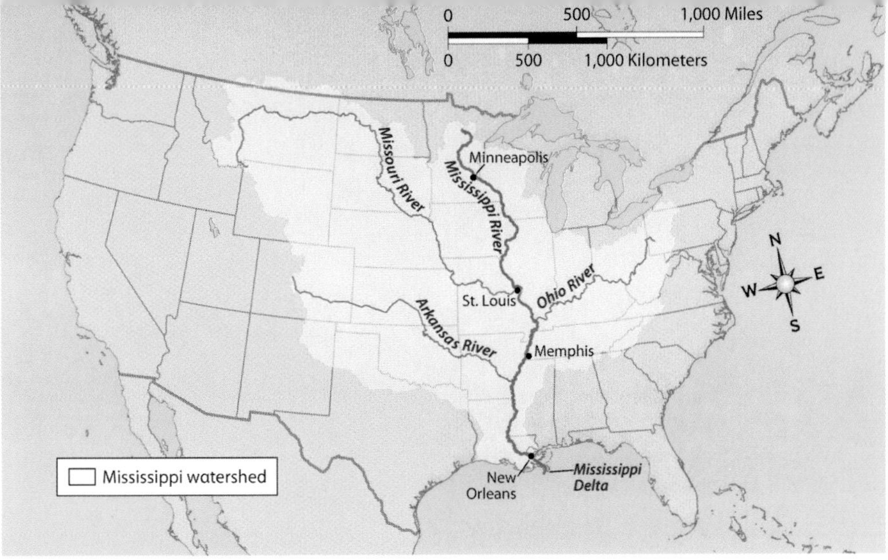

The Mississippi collects water from almost half of the United States.

The Mississippi floods often. Floods move a lot of sediment. Land that is normally dry can be under water. Levees, or ridges of earth, protect nearby towns. The Mississippi can cause major damage if it flows over the levees.

Water changes Earth's surface. It does this through erosion, deposition, and by wearing away rock. Water's might is everywhere. You can see it in the Great Lakes, the Grand Canyon, and the Mississippi River.

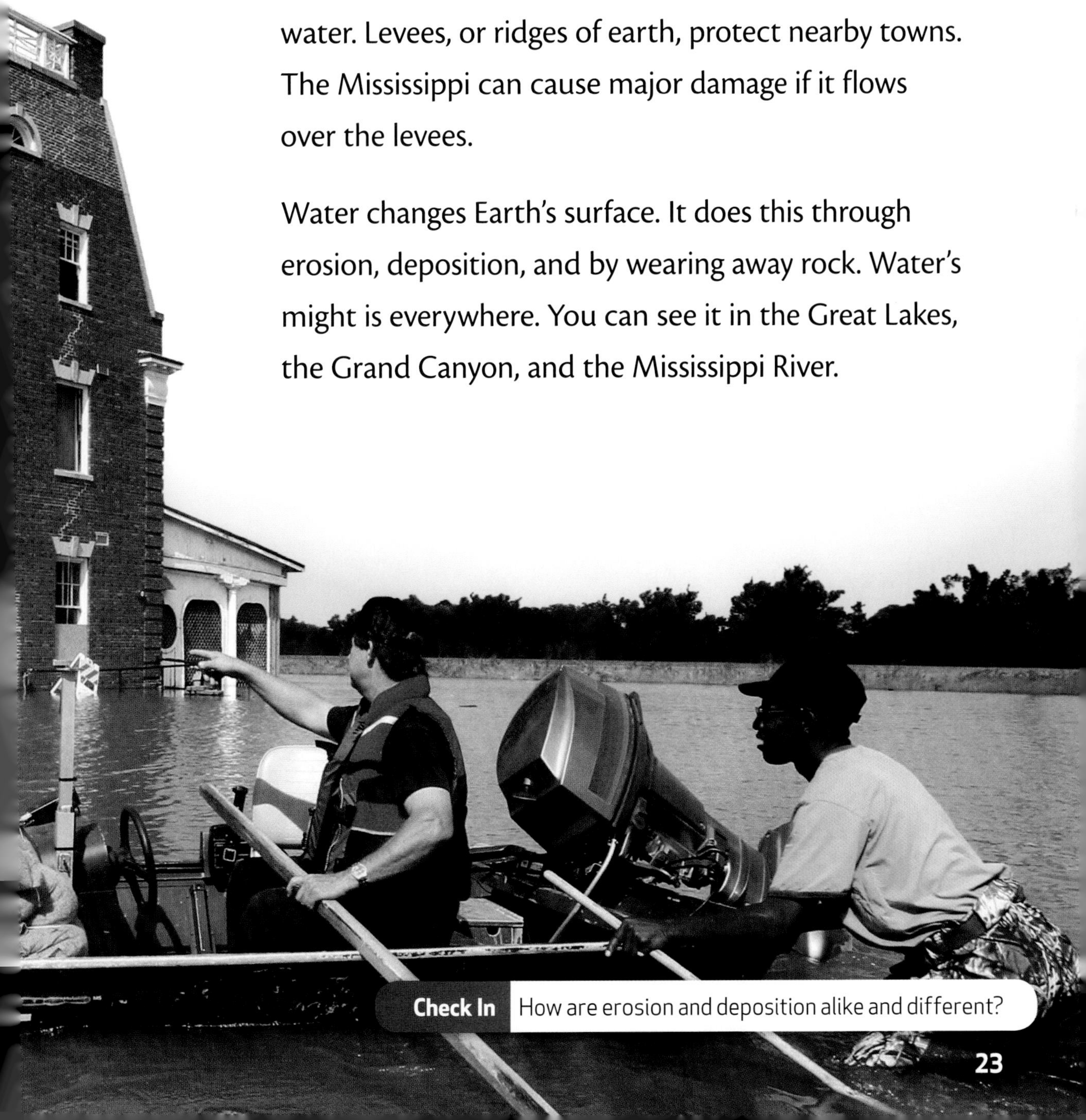

Check In How are erosion and deposition alike and different?

Discuss Characters and Concepts

1. What do you think connects the two pieces that you read in this book? What makes you think that?

2. In "Paul Bunyan and Babe the Blue Ox," explain what events formed the Great Lakes.

3. What do you think is the most important idea in "Water's Might"? What makes you think that? Cite some supporting details.

4. About how long ago did the Colorado River begin to carve out the Grand Canyon? Cite evidence from the text to support your answer.

5. What do you still wonder about Earth's water or landforms? What would be some good ways to find more information?